Literacy Activities for Early Childhood Classrooms

for

Literacy Development in the Early Years
Helping Children Read and Write

Fifth Edition

Lesley Mandel Morrow
The State University of New Jersey

Boston   New York   San Francisco
Mexico City   Montreal   Toronto   London   Madrid   Munich   Paris
Hong Kong   Singapore   Tokyo   Cape Town   Sydney

ISBN 0-205-43946-2

Printed in the United States of America

10 9 8 7 6 5 4 3 2 1   09 08 07 06 05 04

Literacy Activities for Early Childhood Classrooms
Introduction

This supplement provides lesson plans that coincide with each of the ten chapters in the book *Literacy Development in the Early Years: Helping Children Learn to Read and Write, fifth edition.* The plans were written by classroom teachers to provide a model for current exemplary practice in early literacy.

Chapter 1 (p. 1) lays the theoretical foundation for early literacy education. The lesson plans for this chapter are:
- Court is Now in Order
- Have You Ever Had a Bad Idea?

Chapter 2 (p. 3) deals with the assessment of early literacy. The lesson plan for this chapter is:
- Journal Assessment
- Using a Five-Minute Writing Spree to Assess and Teach Word Solving

Chapter 3 (p. 6) addresses issues of diversity in the study of literacy. The two lesson plans for this chapter are:
- Bluebonnet Girl
- Class Storytelling

Chapter 4 (p. 8) presents the topic of language and vocabulary development. The lesson plans include:
- The Five Senses as a Writing Prompt
- Using Word Chunks to Decipher Meaning

Chapter 5 (p. 10) addresses phonological awareness, phonemic awareness, and phonics. The lesson plans are:
- Integrating Phonics Instruction into the Morning Message
- Understanding Homophones

Chapter 6 (p. 12) discusses comprehension. The lesson plans for this chapter are:
- Character Connections
- Recalling Sequential Story Events

Chapter 7 (p.14) focuses upon writing, spelling, and literacy development. The two lesson plans are:
- Script a Play
- Journal Starters

Chapter 8 (p. 16) concentrates upon issues of motivating reading and writing through the use of children's literature. The lesson plans that complement this chapter are:
- A Story Retelling of *The Foot Book* by Dr. Seuss
- A Story Retelling of *The Very Hungry Caterpillar* by Eric Carle
- Letter Writing to Corduroy the Bear

Chapter 9 (p. 19) deals with issues related to organization and management of literacy programs. The lesson plans for this chapter are:
- Finding a "Just Right" Book for Independent Reading
- A Small Group Guided Reading Lesson for Earl Readers: A Sample of Explicit Instruction for Kindergarten – Second Grade

Chapter 10 (p. 22) covers creating strong family literacy partnerships. The two lesson plans for this chapter are:
- Reading Parents
- Pajama Party

Acknowledgements:
I thank the teachers who have generously contributed their time and expertise to designing lessons that support children's literacy development in the early years. I thank Erin Beatty and Kristin Valvanis for gathering the lesson plans and organizing the supplement.

Chapter 1: Foundations of Early Literacy Development

Title: Court is Now in Order

This lesson integrates social studies and literacy instruction. Integrated and theme-oriented instruction emerged during the whole language movement. This lesson may be carried out as a culminating activity for a thematic unit on Fairy Tales.

Objectives: Children will have the opportunity to:
1. Gain knowledge of the various roles played by those involved in the justice system.
2. Take part in constructing a court case based upon information gleaned through literal, inferential, and critical comprehension of a fairy tale.
3. Participate in a mock trial.

Materials: Copy of the story *Goldilocks and the Three Bears*, paper, pencils, and pens for student writing.

Activity:
- Familiarize the students with the fairy tale of *Goldilocks and the Three Bears*. Discuss the various perspectives of each character in the story and how the story could be changed depending upon which story character tells the story. Compare and contrast the story from Goldilocks' and the bears' points of view. This may be done over several days.
- Meanwhile, begin to introduce the students to the different responsibilities of those who work within the judicial system. Include the following: plaintiff, defendant, lawyer, sheriff's officer, court clerk, jury, and judge. You may want to bring in guest speakers from the community. Lawyers came to my class to explain what it is like to be in a courtroom.
- Have each child decide upon a role that they would like to play in the trial of Goldilocks vs. The Three Bears. The roles include the plaintiff (all three bears may participate in the trial), the defendant, at least two lawyers, the sheriff's officer, the court clerk (students may take turns), members of the jury, and the judge who may be played by the principal.
- Prepare for the trial by having the students work together to write the script for the trial. Students must develop questions for the lawyers to ask the witnesses. The witnesses must also be prepared with answers. Make a copy of the final script for each student.
- On the day of the trial, conduct the case using the prepared script. The jury may leave the room to deliberate the verdict and to determine a fair and reasonable punishment if applicable. (The verdict of our case was that Goldilocks was found guilty of vandalism and breaking and entering. Her punishment was to cook porridge for the Three Bears for a week and a $50.00 fine to replace the broken chair.)

Variations:
- Have the children prepare a mock trial for other stories, such as *The Three Little Pigs* or *Little Red Riding Hood*.
- Costumes can be created for the various roles the children assume.
- The children may enjoy hearing *The True Story of the Three Little Pigs* by Jon Scieszka.

Stephanie Zamlong, Second Grade Teacher

Title: Have you ever had a bad idea?

This lesson integrates the IRA/NCTE language arts/literacy standards of reading, writing, listening, speaking, and viewing and is grounded in the social constructivist theoretical tradition. Social constructivism emerged from the work of Lev S. Vygotsky. The theory suggests that literacy events such as reading, writing, and speaking are affected by the individual experiences children and teachers bring to the classroom. This lesson draws on the unique social experiences of children in an effort to motivate literacy development.

Objectives: Children will have the opportunity to:
1. Use prior experiences to develop listening, speaking, and writing skills.
2. Interact with peers.
3. Create a class book.

Materials: Paper, pencils, and pens for student/teacher writing. Optional – copy of the book *The Book of Bad Ideas* by Laura Huliska-Beith

Activity:
- Put the students into pairs.
- Ask the students if they have ever had a bad idea. Model the importance of sharing one that is meant for others to hear. The book *The Book of Bad Ideas* provides a lighthearted read aloud for this topic. Or, if you choose not to use the text, model one of your own. For example, drinking from a cup with a hole in the bottom.
- Explain to students that once they think of an idea, they are going to share this idea with their partners. Emphasize the importance of listening very carefully, because each student will eventually be writing about his/her partner's response.
- Invite students to share ideas. Encourage students to take notes and ask questions to be sure everyone has a good understanding of the conversation. Discuss methods for asking questions to gather more information.
- The students should then individually write about their partner's idea using the information learned from the conversations. These pieces can become part of the writing workshop process.
- When students are ready to submit final copies, create a class anthology.

Variations:
- The same framework could also be used to share a good idea.
- If students aren't writing independently yet, students could dictate individual stories to the teacher.
- Students can work on writing pieces together.
- Illustrations can be added.

Heather Casey, Reading Specialist and Rutgers University Graduate School of Education, Ph.D. Student

Chapter 2: Assessing Early Literacy Development to Design Instruction

Title: Journal Assessment

Objectives: The children will have the opportunity to:
1. Gain an understanding of a rubric.
2. Develop a rubric for journal entries.
3. Utilize a rubric to assess their journal entries.
4. Develop personal goals.

Materials: Chart paper divided into 4 sections, markers, 2-3 journal entries from previous years on overhead transparencies, 5 copies of 2-3 journal entries from previous years which reflect a range of proficiency, students' own journals, pencils.

Activity:
- Review with students the use of their journals and the expectations for entries.
- Explain that they will be working together to decide on a way to evaluate their own journal entries. Introduce the term "rubric."
- Show the students the chart paper, which has been divided into 4 sections. In the first section, write the number "4." Explain that a journal entry that has everything it needs would be given a 4. Work together to decide upon expectations for that type of entry. Be sure to include expectations for illustrations, spaces between words, illustration to text match, and letter formations.
- Write a number "3" in the next box. Explain that this type of journal entry would have most of the expectations met. Work together to describe this type of journal entry.
- Move on to describe a 2 and a 1.
- Using the overhead, display one of the journal entries that you have selected from previous years. Using the established rubric, model evaluating that entry. Follow the same procedure for the other overheads.
- Explain that they will work in groups to evaluate more journal entries. Divide the class into 5 heterogeneous groups and provide each group with copies of the previously selected entries.
- As groups work together, circulate and assist students in utilizing the rubric.
- After each group has completed the task, reconvene as a class and share assessment results.
- Have students find their last journal entry and utilize the rubric to assess their own work, placing a number at the top of the page.
- Students then meet individually with the teacher to discuss their rating and develop their personal goals to improve their journal writing. The teacher or student can write personal goals inside the cover of the student's journal.

Variations:
- This process can be utilized to determine rubrics for any writing project used in the classroom, or for project-based assessment.
- The teacher can design the rubrics in advance.

Suzanne Kazi, Kindergarten Teacher

Title: Using a Five-Minute Writing Spree to Assess and Teach Word Solving

Objectives:
1. Students' knowledge of words will be assessed by writing all the words they can in 5 minutes
2. Students' ability to understand the reading and writing connection will be assessed by observing how they use known words to help them read and write new words.
3. Students' ability to synthesize knowledge of words will be assessed by observing how they derive a new word through analogy to a known word.

Materials: Blank piece of paper (unlined), stop watch, 8 _ x 11" piece of paper folded into 3 or 4 sections, overhead or larger-sized poster of the paper the students have to record words, pre-made personal dictionaries for each student (these can simply be a sheet of 12 x 18" piece of construction paper that can be folded in half and serve as a cover. Each page inside would be for a different letter of the alphabet. You may want to have a picture at the top of the page, next to the letter, so the students have an anchor), magnetic letters may be used in small groups or one-on-one, books on the students instructional level to reinforce the strategy.

Activity:
- Give students (can be in whole group, small group, or one-on-one) a blank sheet of paper
- Say, "Today you are going to write all the words you know." You may need to start with a prompt. "Your name is a word. Can you show me how to write your name? Do you know how to write the names of anyone else in your family or your friends' names?"
- Give students 5-10 minutes to write all the words they know. You may need to provide additional prompts, such as "Do you know how to write any animal words? Do you know you to write words like 'me' or 'my'? Can you write 'mom' or 'dad'? How about words like 'in' or 'it'?"
- After time is up, be sure to praise the child for the work he/she has done. If you are giving the spree in a small or large group, look for commonalities. For example, a majority of the students may be able to write the words "and," "it," and "dad." Look for 3-4 words that most or all of your students can write.
- Provide students with a piece of paper folded into 3 sections.
- Have them write three words that they know at the top of each section of the paper and draw a line under each word. Example: "and," "it," and "dad." You may want to have the same record sheet as an overhead or make a larger version of it using bulletin board paper to display it on the board as a model.
- Read sentences to the students that will encourage them to write new words using known words to assist them. For example: "The teacher asked the students to stand in line for art class." Be sure the students understand the meaning of the word you select and the context in which it is used.
- Ask the students, "What word at the top of your paper will help you write the word 'stand'? Right, 'and' will help you write the word 'stand.' Then 'stand' has the word 'and' in it. Write the word 'stand' under the word 'and' on your paper."
- Continue with several more examples. You may want to have students write 2-4 words under each column.
- Discuss how you can use a known word to write and read a new word.
- Have students create a personal dictionary with words they know. Have a page for each letter of the alphabet. Students record known words alphabetically in their dictionary. Model how to use a personal dictionary when writing independently. This can be stored in their writing folder.

Variations:
- Have more than 3 columns and 3 known words. For example, use "sing," "sang," "song," and "sung." This is especially beneficial for those students who may not be looking carefully at the subtle changes within words.
- Use word wall activities to reinforce word solving by analogy. Provide students with sentences and ask them to find the word on the word wall that will help them spell the word _____.
- After assessing your students using the writing spree in the beginning of the year, record on an index card words most of your students know how to write. Use this as a resource during interactive writing lessons when sharing the pen with students. Model think alouds when using analogies as a strategy during the lesson.
- Use a name chart in the classroom to demonstrate how to use known names of classmates to write new words.
- Use Making Words activities or magnetic letters to reinforce this strategy.
- Reinforce the child's bank of known words and how to use the strategy above during guided reading groups. Use think alouds to demonstrate how to use a known word to help them read a new word at a point of difficulty.

- Continue to reassess your students' progress using the writing spree as a screening tool multiple times a year (example: fall, winter, spring).

Jeanine Heil, Reading Specialist/State Professional Development Coordinator for New Jersey

Chapter 3: Literacy and Diversity: Meeting Individual Needs of English Language Learners, Children with Disabilities and other Diverse Concerns

Title: Bluebonnet Girl

Objectives: The children will have the opportunity to:
1. Learn about Native American culture.
2. Discuss a possession that is important to them.
3. Empathize with a girl from another culture.

Materials: One worksheet per child, drawing and coloring supplies, copy of the book *Bluebonnet Girl* by Michael Lind.

Activity:
- Prepare a worksheet for each child as follows:
- Divide paper in half, leaving space for a drawing on each half. On the first half write "Bluebonnet Girl's precious possession," and on the other half write "Your precious possession."
- Take a picture walk of the book *Bluebonnet Girl*. This will be particularly helpful since aspects of Native American culture will be unfamiliar to the children.
- Read the book.
- Discuss the book with the children. Focus on what is different about the way Native Americans lived to how we live today. Also, discuss what sacrifice the Bluebonnet Girl had to make. Why was her doll special to her?
- Ask the children what their most precious possession is. Why is it important to them? Do a think, pair, share.
- Distribute copies of the worksheet to the students. Have the students illustrate Bluebonnet Girl's precious possession and their own precious possession; they should label illustrations if possible.
- When the worksheet is completed, come back to the group and discuss how they think Bluebonnet Girl felt about giving up her precious possession. How would they feel if they had to do the same?

Variations:
- Students who can write on the topic should be encouraged to do so.
- Have students compare and contrast their precious possession to the Bluebonnet Girl's using a Venn diagram.

Courtney Bell, Rutgers University Graduate School of Education, M.A. Student

Title: Class Storytelling

Objectives: The children will have the opportunity to:
1. Collaborate to create a story in the tradition of oral storytelling.
2. Practice speaking and listening skills (with emphasis on highly expressive language).
3. Examine how individual strengths and differences can be combined to develop a more elaborate, resourceful, and multi-faceted process and/or product.

Materials: Any folktale that invokes the oral storytelling tradition (e.g. Aardema, V. (1983); *Bringing the rain to Kapiti Plain: A Nandi tale*. New York: Puffin; Aardema, V. (1978); *Why mosquitoes buzz in people's ears: A West African tale*. New York: Puffin; Ridgeway, Dawn. (1992); *Does Kakulu's mother use magic?* Windhoek, Namibia: New Namibia Books, Ltd.); small ball; journal; pencil; tape recorder; audiocassette; supplies for drawing.

Activity:
- Set up an audiotape to record the children's story and have the children sit in a big circle.
- As part of a unit on storytelling traditions, read the folktale. Remind the children to listen carefully and pay close attention to how each character contributes to the solution to the problem.
- Lead a discussion about the story based on the idea of combining individual strengths to solve a problem.
- Students will create their own oral story about overcoming challenges with the help of others. One student will hold the ball and start the story with one or two sentences. When the student finishes his/her contribution, he/she will pass the ball to the next person in the circle and that person will continue the story. Monitor the time and if one student goes on for too long, ask the student to pass the ball. At the start of the story, explain that the students should build on each other's ideas while adding their own creativity to the story.
- In their journals, have the children write (or draw) about what they and their neighbor contributed to the complete story.
- Add the recorded class story to the listening center. The students will transcribe and illustrate their portions of the story, which will be combined and bound into a class book.

Variations:
- The children can stand in a circle with a bunch of props in the middle. As they create the story, they may incorporate props and movements into their storytelling.
- Students will contribute based on their abilities. Students who struggle with expressive language can provide shorter segments of the story. Students who need to be more challenged can give longer and more elaborate segments of the story.

Julie Anastasi and Courtney Bell, Rutgers University Graduate School of Education, M.A. Students

Chapter 4: Language and Vocabulary Development

Title: The Five Senses as a Writing Prompt

Objectives: The children will have the opportunity to:
1. Use background knowledge to generate ideas for a story.
2. Fill in a web and a story elements chart to organize information.
3. Work in cooperative small groups to develop a story.
4. Understand how sensory stimulation can activate prior knowledge.

Materials: *Vision*—ex: a picture without words or any object; *hearing*—ex: a sound effect or song; *touch*—ex: sandpaper or velvet; *taste*—ex: honey or lemon; *smell*—ex: pine or watermelon scent; writing supplies; photocopies of a web and story elements charts for student use

Activity:
- Discuss how our five senses can help us to recall background information.
- Provide students with an example of how this can happen by letting them know what you think of when you smell a certain scent. Prompt them to share what comes to their minds.
- On the board or on chart paper, model the use of a web to organize their thoughts and ideas.
- Instruct the class that they will be divided into five small groups and that each group will receive a different sensory stimulus. After *seeing, hearing, touching, tasting,* or *smelling,* each student will use a web to organize his or her thoughts. Once they have completed their web, they will share them with their small groups. Afterwards, they will work collaboratively to develop a story using ideas generated from their webs.
- Divide the children into small groups. Distribute a web for each student and a story elements chart for each group.
- As you provide the *hearing, touching, tasting,* and *smelling* groups with their sensory stimulation, have them close their eyes to enhance their experiences.
- After all stories have been written, form a circle in the carpet area as a whole group. Have each of the five small groups share their experiences of the sensory stimulation and their story with the rest of the class. Reveal the objects used to stimulate their senses.

Variations:
- Rotate groups so that all children experience stimulation through each of the five senses.
- Instead of writing a story, students may work individually or in cooperative small groups to create a poem.
- Ask the class to bring in objects from their home for each of the fives senses to be used for this writing activity.
- Younger students can simply discuss or draw pictures of what comes to their minds for each sensory stimulus.

Maridy Gamoso, Rutgers University Graduate School of Education, M.A. Student

Title: Using Word Chunks to Decipher Meaning

Objectives: The children will have the opportunity to:
1. Look for known chunks or small words to attempt to decode an unknown word.
2. Use grade-appropriate dictionaries with assistance from the teacher.

Materials: Copies of the book *The Stories Julian Tells* by Ann Cameron (one per student), paper divided into three columns: "Words I Don't Know," "My Meaning," "Dictionary Meaning" (one sheet per student), writing materials.

Activity:
- After reading "Catalog Cats" in *The Stories Julian Tells*, discuss with students why Julian told Huey that a *catalog* is a book with real cats in it (because the big word *catalog* has the smaller word *cat* in it).
- Tell students that even though Julian made up a silly meaning for *catalog* to trick Huey, he used a good strategy. Huey was faced with a big word he did not know the meaning of, so Julian used the smaller words found in the big word to make up a new definition.
- Present students with several words (i.e., *butterfly*, *ladybug* or *handkerchief*) and ask them what silly meaning Julian might come up with. Then discuss what the words really mean (you can model looking up words in the dictionary if students need to be reminded about what to do).
- Distribute the papers for defining words and ask students to reread "Catalog Cats" making a list of the words they do not know the meaning of in the first column. In the second column ("My Meaning") they should look for smaller words in the words on their list and come up with their own definitions. Lastly, they should use the class dictionaries to look up the words and write the correct meaning in the third column ("Dictionary Meaning"), taking note of whether or not their definition matches the one in the dictionary.
- When students have finished, have them share one or two words from their list with another student. As class, talk about how this was helpful. Did this strategy work for some words and not for others? (Generally works best for compound words like *handkerchief*. Using this for non-compound words, like *catalog* might result in some very silly definitions.)

Variations:
- Students can look for smaller words within a larger word to help them discover the meaning of unknown words in any story they read.

Jennifer Durkin, Rutgers University Graduate School of Education, M.A. Student

Chapter 5: Strategies to Figure Out Words: Phonological Awareness, Phonemic Awareness, and Phonics

Title: Integrating Phonics Instruction into the Morning Message

Objectives: Children will have the opportunity to:
1. Learn how knowledge of word families facilitates decoding of words.
2. Use context clues as a means of decoding unknown words.

Materials: Chart paper, markers, sticky notes.

Activity:
- Compose a morning message on scrap paper that uses the words from the "at" word family. Circle the words that belong to the "at" family and then cross out the initial consonant. For example: *Sylvester was here, he sat on the rug. We will sit on our mats while John shows his cat. This will be fun!*
- Re-write the message onto chart paper, omitting the initial consonant of all the "at" family words. Example: *Today we will have John's _at visit our classroom. The last time Sylvester was here, he _at on the rug. We will sit on our _ats while John shows us his _at. This will be fun!*
- Show the Morning Message to the students, explaining that letters are missing. Read the message aloud, encouraging the children to read along. Everyone claps when they come across a missing letter.
- To begin the process for problem-solving the unknown words, ask the children to tell you what information the DO know after reading the first sentence of the message. Students may, for example, say "Something is visiting," or, "It's something that belongs to John."
- Based upon the known information, generate a list of possible letters that would make sense in the missing space. As students respond, write their guesses onto a sticky note and place it in the blank in order to provide a visual link for problem solving.
- Ask students what the best choice would be. Write the correct letter onto the chart. Have the students read the sentence to check if it makes sense and sounds right. Repeat these steps with the remainder of the morning message.
- When all the blanks are filled with the correct letters, read the complete message. You may have the class read chorally, or you may select a few students to read.

Variations:
- As children become more adept at applying word analysis skills, you may focus on more than one word family within a morning message. You may also misspell words and eliminate punctuation and ask the children to identify the errors.

Jeanne Velechko, Third Grade Teacher

Title: Understanding Homophones

Objectives: Children will have the opportunity to:
1. Identify homophones.
2. Demonstrate understanding of when each word in a pair of homophones should be used.

Materials: Index cards (one per student for every homophone pair presented in the lesson), markers, sentence strips with pre-written sentences that contain each word of a homophone pair.

Activity:
- Create a list of easily confused homophones. The list should include the homophones your students spell incorrectly when writing. Some possibilities include:

Its	it's	
To	too	two
There	their	they're

- Introduce the term "homophone" by explaining that at times we hear words that sound the same, but are spelled differently. Emphasize the need to use the correct spelling, since it affects the meaning of a sentence.
- Provide a model by showing and reading aloud two sentence strips that each contains one word of a pair of homophones. For example, Strip 1 will read, "I have a bee buzzing around me!" Strip 2 will read, "Will you be at my party?"
- Have the students identify the pair of homophones. Discuss spelling and meaning differences between the homophones.
- Have the students write the homophones (*be* and *bee*) onto an index card, one word on each side of the card.
- Continue by reading another sentence strip that contains one word of the pair. This time, do not allow the students to see the sentence.
- Instruct the students to hold up their index card so that it indicates the form of the homophone they expect to see in the sentence. Show the sentence strip and discuss the correct answer.
- Repeat this process using several sentences.

Variations:
- When teaching sight word vocabulary, children can use scrap paper cut to the size of index cards to write sight words. Say the word, have the students write it onto their paper, and hold it up for a quick class check.

Jeanne Velechko, Third Grade Teacher

Chapter 6: Developing Comprehension of Text and Concepts about Books

Title: Character Connections

Objectives: The children will have the opportunity to:
1. Provide literal recall of a character and his or her actions in a book.
2. Make inferential judgments about a character's behavior.
3. Make personal connections with a character.

Materials: 2 _ sheets of 8 _" by 11" paper per child, supplies for drawing: markers, crayons, pencils.

Activity:
- Prepare a master copy of the pages for the character activity as follows:
- Divide each sheet in half. You should have five rectangles.
- On the first sheet, make a cover titled "My Book About _____". Add spaces for the book title, author and illustrator's names, and child's name.
- On the second half-sheet, write, "What _____ looks like."
- On the third half-sheet, write, "What _____ does."
- On the fourth half-sheet, write, "_____ would like to…"
- On the fifth, write, "_____ is like me because…"
- Photocopy enough copies for each child and then cut and staple the books in order.
- Instruct the children to select one character from a shared story. Have them add the character's name to the front cover, along with the other information requested.
- Model creating a character book by walking through each page. Demonstrate how to look through text to determine what the character looks like and does (pages 2 and 3), deciding what the character might do if he or she were real (page 4), and how the character is like them (page 5).
- Have the students create their character book by using pictures, print, or a combination thereof.
- Allow time for a whole class or small group sharing of the character books.

Variations:
- The students may write paragraphs using the information from their books to describe their character. These can be presented as dramatic narratives where the children dress like the character and orally present their paragraphs.
- The same format can be applied to reading expository texts. Children may create a book that demonstrates their comprehension and degree of understanding about factual material.
- Children may create books that depict the sequence of events in a story in order to help them internalize story structure.

Margaret G. Niemiec, Reading Specialist

Title: Recalling Sequential Story Events

Objectives: The children will have the opportunity to:
1. Recall the events of a story in sequential order.
2. Use a graphic organizer (story wheel) to help with comprehension.
3. Recognize and delineate setting, characters, plot development, and resolution.

Materials: A blank copy of the story wheel for each child, pencils, erasers, a copy of the story for reference.

Activity:
- After reading the story (either as a whole group or in smaller reading groups), briefly discuss what children remember (setting, characters, plot, etc.).
- Explain to them that they will be filling out a story wheel. Show them a blank copy, review what each section says, and ask them to give an example of how to fill in the blanks.
- Distribute story wheels – a sheet of paper with a large circle broken into four numbered sections:
- Section one states, "The story takes place _____. The characters are _____.First, _____."
- Section two states, "Then, _____."
- Section three says, "Things began to change when _____."
- The fourth section says, "Finally, _____."
- In the first section, students should identify the setting, characters and first main event.
- In the second section, students should identify the next main event (perhaps new characters are introduced, depending on the story)
- In the third, they should write down the focus problem/turning point.
- In the final section of the wheel, students identify the resolution.
- Throughout the activity, elicit students' ideas.
- Allow time for students to share/compare their answers.

Variations:
- Use the story wheel to assess comprehension of one aspect of the story, such as a single character. Have students describe the character's feelings/situations as s/he develops throughout the story.
- Use the story wheel as a more formal assessment tool for comprehension.

Stephanie Schraeter, Rutgers University Graduate Student, M.A. Student

Chapter 7: Writing, Spelling, and Literacy Development

Title: Script a Play

Objectives: Children will have the opportunity to:
1. Develop their writing abilities while working cooperatively.
2. Practice writing dialog that incorporates expressive language and correct punctuation associated with writing speech.

Materials: A variety of dress-up clothes and props (purses, briefcases, etc.), writing paper and pencils.

Activity:
- Send children in small groups to the area of the room where the dress-up clothes and props are located. Allow the children time to explore the items in order to decide which props they would like to use and what clothing they would like to wear as a costume. The children then decide which character they would like to play.
- Together the children compose a story that includes the character each created. Each child writes the story so that each one has his or her own copy of the script.
- Once the play is written, the children show it to the teacher. Suggestions may be made for editing and revising.
- The children then dress in their costumes to rehearse and dramatize the play. On occasion, plays may be performed for the class or for another appreciative audience.

Variations:
- Costumes, puppets, or masks that relate to storybook characters may be placed in the dress-up area along with corresponding pieces of literature. The children may write plays based upon these familiar characters and stories.

Fran Regis, First Grade Teacher

Title: Journal Starters

Objectives: Children will have the opportunity to:
1. Develop a tool that is self-selected and easily accessible for prompting journal writing.

Materials: Pocket folders (one per student), scissors, magazines, newspapers, old calendars, other sources of pictures, and markers.

Activity:
- Give the students each a folder and ask them to label it with their names and decorate it as desired using the markers.
- Explain to the students that they will be writing in their journals on a daily basis. There may be days when they have difficulty thinking of a topic on which to write. Therefore, they are going to create a folder of pictures they can use whenever they need an idea to spark their writing.
- Provide students with the various magazines and newspapers from which to select and cut out pictures that interest them. Pictures are then placed in the folders.
- Encourage the children to bring in photographs or pictures from home to add to their folder at any point in the school year.

Variations:
- The children's picture collections may also be used to spark story writing or used as illustrations for stories children have written.

Jennifer Haik, Second Grade Teacher

Chapter 8: Motivating Reading and Writing Using Children's Literature, Literacy Centers, Technology, and Play

Title: A Story Retelling of *The Foot Book* by Dr. Seuss

Objectives: Children will have the opportunity to:
1. Participate in re-enacting the story by creating a slide show.
2. Extend their understanding of opposites specific to *The Foot Book*.

Materials: A copy of the text, camera and slide film, props (socks, clown costume, water, towel, bandages, stuffed cat, stuffed guinea pig, chair, ladder, ball), poster-making materials (paper, poster board, letter stencils).

Activity:
- Read *The Foot Book* to the children.
- List the different slide pictures they are going to create by telling them that the pictures in the book will relate to the pictures they will be re-enacting.
- Assign children to specific pages. Have the children offer ideas and make a list of the props they will need for their picture of the re-enactment.
- Have the children make the posters for their page using the poster board, letter stencils, and markers. Emphasize the opposite words in the story.
- Photograph the children as they pose with their props and posters just like their assigned page in the book.
- Show the slide story while having the children re-tell each page as it appears on the screen. Have the children use different tones of voice when reading the opposite word pairs.

Variations:
- Mount photographs reproduced from the slides into a special classroom edition of *The Foot Book*. Place it in your classroom library for the children to retell the story.
- Create a pack of cards that includes opposite words from *The Foot Book*. Have children match the opposite words. Include blank cards for children to record their own opposite pairs. These can later be put into a class book of opposites to go along with the class rendition of *The Foot Book*.

Pat Carroll and Amy Natus, Rutgers University Graduate School of Education, M.A. Student

Title: A Story Retelling of *The Very Hungry Caterpillar* by Eric Carle

Objectives: The children will have the opportunity to:
1. Retell the story in sequential order.
2. Identify the days of the week and the number words "one" through "five."
3. Gain an understanding of the lifecycle of a butterfly.

Materials: A copy of the text, the following laminated construction paper story-telling props: one apple, two pears, three plums, four strawberries, five oranges, one leaf, a variety of junk food, a cocoon, and butterfly wings. Place a strip of magnetic tape onto the back of each prop. (In most cases, these will stick to the chalkboard in your classroom. If not, try a metal stovetop cover. It works great!) Also, days of the week and number words "one" through "five" written onto index cards.

Activity:
- Tell the story using the props. Invite the children to join you in the storytelling by emphasizing the story pattern and encouraging them to say the repetitive phrase.
- Use the props to review the sequence of the story as well as the days of the week and number of items eaten on a particular day.
- Guide the children in matching the days-of-the-week cards and the number word cards to the item(s) eaten. Model how to use the beginning letter of each word to decode it. Show how to check it by running their fingers under each letter of the word and making sure they have a sound for each letter. Point out the repetitive "day" chunk in each of the weekday words.
- Place the storytelling materials along with the word cards into the classroom literacy center to allow for independent and partner retellings of the story.

Variations:
- Have the children look through magazines and newspaper circulars to find pictures of the items that the caterpillar ate. The children can make their own little book of the story by pasting the pictures onto pages where they write the day of the week and the number word of each item consumed.

Kriaki Sklavounos, First Grade Teacher

Title: Letter Writing to Corduroy the Bear

Objectives: The children will have the opportunity to:
1. Learn about the parts of an informal letter.
2. Apply that knowledge by writing a letter to Corduroy.

Materials: A copy of the book *Corduroy* and *A Pocket for Corduroy* by Don Freeman, chart paper to record students' responses, large mailbox, "Letterman," (see diagram), letter from Corduroy written on large chart paper, paper envelopes, pencils for letter writing, stuffed Corduroy bear.

Activity:
- Over a period of two days, read aloud the Corduroy books. Model some things you would like to ask Corduroy or say to him if you had the chance. Have the children offer the same while you record their statements and questions onto chart paper.
- After school on the second day, Corduroy "visits" your classroom and leaves a big mailbox, a stuffed Corduroy, and a letter saying "Dear Boys and Girls, I am so happy that you are reading stories about me. Since we can't talk in person, you can write a letter to me and I'll write back! Love, Corduroy."
- Explain to the children that they must first learn how to write a letter in order to correspond with Corduroy. Introduce "Letterman," who will "save the day" by showing them how it's done. "Letterman" displays the three parts of a letter: the heading, the body, and the closing.

- Explain and model each part by writing a sample letter to Corduroy. Refer to the comments and questions generated on the two previous days.
- Give students the opportunity to write to Corduroy by following the model.
- "Mail" the letters and enjoy the fun when the children get a response from Corduroy. (Older students love reading and answering the letters that the children write to Corduroy. It's an authentic letter writing activity for them, too.)

Variations:
- The children may also enjoy listening to *The Jolly Possum* by Janet and Allan Ahlberg.
- Find a class of older students to be in-school pen pals with your students. Encourage letter writing on a regular basis.
- Introduce the children to e-mail letter writing.

Angela Feola, Second Grade Teacher

Chapter 9: Organizing and Managing the Literacy Program

Title: Finding a "Just Right" Book for Independent Reading

Objectives: The children will have the opportunity to:
1. Gain understanding of different levels of text and how that affects their reading.
2. Practice identifying books that are within their independent reading level.

Materials: A variety of leveled books that represent a wide span of levels, a pan balance, objects to be weighed, photocopies of blank pan balances for student use.

Activity:
This portion of the lesson is carried out in a whole class context:
- In pairs, have the students share with each other things that they find very easy to do and activities that they find very challenging. Model by sharing something that's easy for you and something that you find very hard to carry out.
- After a few minutes of sharing, reconvene as a whole group and discuss the topic. Highlight the fact that things that are easy for one may not be easy for another and vice versa.
- Show the pan balance. Explain how the pan balance shows the heaviness of an object. Describe how activities that are too hard leave you feeling "weighed down," like the pan balance with heavy weight. Activities that are too easy can represent the pan balance that is suspended in the air. "There's nothing to it." Then display the pan balance with equivalent weights. Explain how it is perfectly balanced or "just right."
- Have the children return to their pairs and work together to complete the diagrams of the pan balances by writing their hard activities on the low pan, their easy activities on the high pan, and their "just right" activities in the middle.

The following portion of the lesson takes place in small groups:
- Review the concept of the pan balance as it relates to things people do. Explain that it also relates to books. Show samples of texts that are too hard. Discuss their qualities (too many words, no pictures, too many words that need decoding, etc.). Place them on the pan balance so the pan lowers dramatically.
- Do the same with books that are too easy. Place fewer of them in the pan balance so they are significantly lighter. Remove the books from the balance.
- Then discuss "just right" books by describing the specific characteristics for which the children should be looking. Place them on the scale so that both sides are equivalent in weight.
- Have each child apply the information by looking for a "just right" book. Monitor their process.

Note: A poster depicting a balanced scale and the words "Just Right" may serve as a reminder to the students.

Danielle D. Lynch, Kindergarten Teacher

Title: A Small Group Guided Reading Lesson for Early Readers: A Sample of Explicit Instruction for Kindergarten – Second Grade

Objectives: The Children will have the opportunity to:
1. Engage in a small group lesson crafted to their individual needs as developing readers.
2. Develop the strategies necessary for independent reading.

Materials: One copy per student of a text selected for its inherent qualities that will allow for skill and strategy instruction. (Note: The text must be in the instructional reading level of the children. That means the children should be able to read 90-94% of the text accurately and with good comprehension prior to the lesson.) Additional useful materials: White boards and markers for teacher and student use, magnetic letters, chart paper on a stand.

A Guided Reading Lesson Format:
The text used in this sample lesson is *Tricky Tracy* published by Rigby. In this story, a girl named Tracy plays tricks on others by pretending to be in trouble. Shortly, those around her realize that she is not in need of assistance when she asks. One day, her trick backfires and she really does need help. This time, no one comes to her aid.

*   **Introduction to the Text**: Generate a <u>brief</u> conversation that stimulates the children's background knowledge related to the text.
*   "Have you ever played a trick on anyone? Did that person you tricked think it was funny? Did you ever have someone play a trick on you that you didn't like?"
*   **Book Walk or Picture Walk**: Guide the children through the text by discussing the text illustrations. You may walk through the entire text or choose only certain pages to discuss. Bring forward any concepts related to comprehending the text that you think might be new or challenging for the children in the group. The book walk should be tailored to the needs of the children.
*   In *Tricky Tracy,* you may discuss the worried looks on the characters' faces when they thought that Tracy was in trouble. Have the children hypothesize how they think the characters felt when they learned she was only tricking.
*   Word work may be integrated into the book walk. You may ask the children to locate certain words or apply problem-solving strategies together before having the children read the book independently.
*   In this text, some children have difficulty with the words "only" and "always." Discussing the strategy of looking for known "chunks" in an unknown word and applying it to decoding these two words may be useful.
*   **Children Read the Text Independently and Silently**: Set a purpose for reading and instruct the children to begin. While they read, circulate among the group members asking them to quietly read aloud when you crouch next to them. If the children are not yet ready to read silently, instruct them to read very quietly. Make sure the children understand that they are not to read chorally. Circulate among the group and listen-in on individual readers.
*   **Individual Strategy Instruction:** As you listen to individual children read, prompt their thinking toward developing reading strategies. Respond to their miscues in such a way that they learn to synthesize all the information sources readers use. The following examples offer suggestions of such prompts:
*   When children miscue by making a meaningless substitution, you may say, "Does that make sense? Look at the picture. Would that be right? Think about what you read so far. Would that belong in this story?"
*   When children miscue by not monitoring their language use, you can ask, "Does that sound right? Do we talk like that? Listen to what you read (you repeat). What doesn't sound right about it?"
*   When children fail to use the letters in a word as an information source, you can ask, "Does that look right? Point and check if you have a sound for every letter? Is there a little word in the big word that you know?"
*   Be sure to praise self-correction, the use of self-monitoring strategies, expressive reading, and fluency.
*   If the children are reading short texts, you may ask them to read it again. You may also instruct them to read with a partner. This will give you additional time to do individual instruction.
*   **Group Instruction**: Based upon your assessment and observation of the children as they read the text, conduct a mini-lesson based on their needs. This may include compound words, suffixes, prefixes, punctuation, rhyming words, fluency, comprehension skills such as inferencing, etc.

- **Follow-Up:** Not every book used in a guided reading lesson is followed by an activity. Some may lend themselves to artistic or dramatic connections that enhance the story meaning. Most often, follow-up simply consists of taking the book home to re-read it, placing it in a book basket for independent reading, or being assigned new pages to read which will be discussed the next time the group meets.

Elizabeth Asbury, Reading Specialist, Learning Consultant

Chapter 10: Family Literacy Partnerships: Home and School Working Together

Title: Reading Parents

Objectives: The children will have the opportunity to:
1. Develop fluency in oral reading.
2. Increase confidence and comfort in reading by developing a one-on-one relationship with a parent volunteer.

Materials: A cozy corner for the parent volunteer and student to read together, books selected by the teacher or students for reading to the parent.

Activity:
- Introduce the idea of Reading Parents at Back-to-School Night. Determine which parents are interested in reading with children individually or in small groups throughout the school year. Make up a schedule of volunteers providing them with a day and time that they will come to read aloud or hear the children read to them. Group the children according to the parents' schedules so they become Monday readers, Tuesday Readers, etc.
- When the parent arrives, s/he goes to the designated reading area. The first child who is prepared to read proceeds to the reading area. After reading with the parent for about 5 minutes, the child quietly lets the next child know it is their turn to read. When all the children have read, the parent can quietly leave with little or no interruption to the class routine.
- You may choose to assign a small book for reading, such as a vowel-intensive story or a theme-related book, before the children begin to make their own book choices. This allows the teacher to have the children work on a specific skill are in their reading.
- The parents do not have to keep any written record of the children's progress but often like to quietly comment to me about the great improvement they see in the children as the year progresses. Parents may be asked to keep a reading log for each child wherein they record the book title and author and can make additional comments about the session.

Suggestions for Success:
Meet with all the Reading Parents before the start of the program. Discuss the following points:
- The need to remain positive toward the children at all times.
- Make them aware that the children assigned to them will be on different reading levels. It is imperative that they do not discuss any child's ability with another parent outside the school setting.
- Non-readers can be read to until they have made enough progress to do their own reading.
- Discuss effective ways to help children who "get stuck" on words and need assistance.

Joan M. Robinson, Kindergarten Teacher

Title: A Pajama Party! A Great Event to Spark School, Family, & Community Literacy Partnerships

The "Pajama Party" is an event in which the children and teachers who choose to participate come to school for the evening dressed for bed, carrying a blanket, a favorite stuffed animal, and a favorite book. We hold this once-a-year event for kindergarten and first grade students and their parents and have a standing-room only crowd in the school library.

The children meet in the gymnasium to sing songs, and listen to a storyteller. While the children enjoy story time, the parents are with the reading specialist whose main goal for the evening is to educate parents on the value of reading to their children on a daily basis. Good read alouds are modeled, books shown and enjoyed, parental concerns and questions addressed, and a healthy attitude toward reading with children is nurtured.

When the parents return to the gym they sit with their child and enjoy a story from the storyteller. Then the parents snuggle up with their children and read aloud a favorite book. We finish the evening with a "bedtime" snack of milk and cookies.

We tried many things to boost parental involvement with mediocre results prior to initiating The Pajama Party. We have experienced great success in getting parents to participate in this annual event. It has become a tradition that is anticipated by all.

A Sample Agenda for the Parent Meeting

The 30-minute parent meeting takes place in the school library. While the parents meet, the children remain in the gymnasium with the teachers.

Objectives: The parents will have the opportunity to:
1. Gain understanding into the role that they play in facilitating their child's reading development
2. Become familiar with practical strategies they can use to support reading development.

Activity:
- Begin by reading aloud a trade book. You may want to consider *Time for Bed* by Mem Fox in order to model a read-aloud bedtime story. Demonstrate how to read expressively, how to ask questions to get children thinking as they listen, etc.
- Share the importance of reading aloud. I have an overhead that reads, "The most important thing you can do for your child? READ ALOUD!"
- Discuss ways to find good books for reading aloud. The following resources may be helpful to parents: teachers; school and public librarians; book stores that have large children's literature sections as well as knowledgeable personnel; children's magazines; etc.
- Show books that have qualities that relate specifically to the needs of early readers. Explain how repetition and rhyme support developing readers. You may want to model using *Love You Forever* by Robert Munsch.
- Give parents an easy-to-understand overview of the reading process. You may want to discuss the three cueing systems (visual, meaning, and structural) and give examples of how to prompt for each.
- Or you may prefer sharing a few practical ideas for how parents can help at home with early through fluent readers. For example, offer suggestions for how to help children decode words. Or explain why story retellings are important and demonstrate how to prompt children to engage in a retelling.
- Allow time to entertain questions.
- Close by interactively reading a poem with the parents. *Read to Me* by Jane Yolen is perfect!
- The parents then return to the gymnasium to enjoy a storytelling, read with their child, and have a "bedtime" snack.

Note: Make sure the parents realize that they must stay the entire time. This is not a "real" sleepover, and the parents do not need to come in their p.j.'s.

A Sample Agenda for the Students

The children stay with the teachers in the gymnasium as the parents proceed to the library for the parent presentation. The entire Pajama Party lasts about one hour.

Objectives: The children will have the opportunity to:
1. Engage in activities that promote literacy development in the motivational context of a large group.
2. Engage in interactive reading with a parent.

Activity:
- Greet the children as they arrive, and pass out color-coded teddy bear nametags. Children are grouped by the color of their tag. The children sit with the teacher who is holding the teddy bear that matches their nametag color.
- Dance "The Hokey Pokey." Children form circles or double lines with their group members. You may want to use a tape-recorded version of the song.
- Dramatize the "Teddy Bear, Teddy Bear, Turn Around" rhyme while chanting it aloud and reading it from an overhead projector. Select one or two children from each group to be the "shadow bears" who model the movements.
- Storytelling presentation – if you are unable to get a storyteller, you may use the following as an alternative format:
- Read aloud *Mooncake* by Frank Ashe. While one teacher reads, another points to the text that has been printed onto overhead transparencies.
- Gather the children into a large circle. One teacher leads "I'm Going on a Bear Hunt" as the other teachers participate and interact with the children.
- The parents return to the gymnasium. They enjoy a final story from the guest storyteller. Then they read aloud to their children and together enjoy a "bedtime" snack.

Lynette Brenner, Reading Specialist

NOTES

NOTES

NOTES

NOTES